# Cornerstones of Freedom

# The Story of

# GERONIMO

By Zachary Kent

CHILDRENS PRESS®
CHICAGO

Library of Congress Cataloging-in-Publication Data

Kent, Zachary.
    The story of Geronimo / by Zachary Kent.
        p.    cm. — (Cornerstones of freedom)
    Summary: A biography of the Apache warrior who led attacks on
settlers and soldiers in Mexico and the Southwestern United States
during the 1870s and 1880s.
    ISBN 0-516-04743-4
    1.  Geronimo, Apache Chief, 1829-1909.   2.   Apache Indians—
Biography—Juvenile literature.   3.   Indians of North America—
Southwest, New—Biography—Juvenile literature.   [1.  Geronimo,
Apache Chief, 1829-1909.   2.   Apache Indians—
Biography.   3.   Indians of North America—
Biography.]   I. Title.   II.  Series.
E99.A6G3245   1989
970.004'97—dc19                                          88-37005
[B]                                                      CIP
[92]                                                     AC

Geronimo! Geronimo was on the loose! Terror gripped the people of the American Southwest in the spring of 1886. Nervous telegraph operators tapped out the alarm; newspaper headlines screamed for action. Geronimo, the fiercest Apache, had escaped from the San Carlos Indian Reservation with a band of followers. The U.S. Army seemed powerless to capture him.

As word spread, frightened Arizona and New Mexico farmers barred doors and boarded up windows. Through lonely nights, anxious cowboys peered in the dark, guarding their grazing herds. In the mountains prospectors packed their mules and hurried toward the safety of towns.

In April the dreaded Apaches struck. Creeping near the village of Calabasas, Arizona, they stole some horses. Then riding to the Peck family ranch a few miles away they murdered Mrs. Peck, her thirteen-year-old child, and a ranch hand named Owens. During the next days the outlaw Indians roved the countryside leaving behind eleven dead ranchers. Terrified citizens claimed at least 150 savage Apaches were on the rampage. In reality Geronimo traveled with only twenty men and another twenty women and children.

Crossing into Mexico's Sierra Madre mountains in June 1886, the little Apache band continued its guerrilla war. "...We ranged in the mountains...for some time," declared Geronimo afterwards. "...whenever Mexican freighters passed we killed them, took what supplies we wanted, and destroyed the remainder. We were reckless of our lives, because we felt that everyman's hand was against us. If we returned to the reservation we would be put in prison and killed...so we gave no quarter to anyone and asked no favors." After a lifetime of warfare, perhaps Geronimo guessed that this was his peoples' last great bid for freedom.

For a thousand years the Apaches had roamed the mountains and plains of the American Southwest. The Nednis clan of the Chiricahua Apache Indian group often camped near the headwaters of the Gila River in what is now Arizona. It was there that a baby was born sometime in the 1820s named Goyahkla meaning "One Who Yawns." The yawning child would become famous by his Spanish name, Geronimo. "This range was our fatherland," Geronimo later exclaimed. "Among these mountains our wigwams were hidden; the scattered valleys contained our fields; the boundless prairies, stretching away on every side, were our pastures; the rocky caverns were our burying places."

Apache family on horseback gathers acorns.

Apache men hunted deer, antelope, and elk, while the women gathered nuts, plucked berries from the bushes, and collected melons and corn. To survive, the Apaches evolved into a fiercely warlike group. Apache raiders attacked neighboring Indian groups as well as the Mexicans who gradually settled in the region. The Apaches stole horses and cattle to satisfy their needs.

As a boy, Geronimo learned Apache skills. Rising early, he ran for hours, as if his life depended upon his speed and strength. He learned to make bows and practiced shooting arrows at targets. He raced ponies across the plains and, as a teenager, joined the hunting parties of the Apache men. Other times he trained for war—wrestling, dodging lances, hiding, tracking. Geronimo explored the hills and prairies until he knew every trail and spring of water.

After winning the Mexican War in 1848, the United States took possession of the Arizona and New Mexico territories. The Apaches watched with suspicion as American surveyors and mining expeditions edged into their homelands.

For Geronimo, this was a time of growth as an Apache warrior. Four times the young Apache took part in raids with the older men. When he was admitted into the warriors' council, Geronimo was permitted to marry.

He chose a pretty, slender girl named Alope. "I...made for us a new home," he recalled. "The tepee was made of buffalo hides and in it were many bear robes, lion [cougar] hides, and other trophies of the chase, as well as my spears, bows, and arrows. Alope...was a good wife....We followed the traditions of our fathers and were happy. Three children came to us—children that played...and worked as I had done."

Apache women in front of their home.

Tragedy robbed Geronimo of his happiness. Often his Apache clan wandered south into Mexico. Near the town of Janos in the 1850s, the Apache camp was suddenly attacked by Mexican soldiers. The surprised Indian men, women, and children in camp were killed.

"I found that. . .my young wife and my three small children were among the slain," mourned Geronimo.

Returning to the Gila River, Geronimo grieved over the massacre of his family. "I was never again contented," he declared. "...Whenever I...saw anything to remind [me] of former days my heart would ache for revenge upon Mexico."

The following year the hate-filled Geronimo led a large war party back to Mexico. Church bells rang the alarm as the Apache warriors approached the little town of Arizpe. During the next two days, the Mexican garrison at Arizpe charged the encircling Apaches repeatedly. One warrior in particular attracted the Mexicans' attention. He wildly ran among them in the confusion of battle, shooting his arrows and slashing with his knife. Standing five feet eight inches in height, with his dark eyes gleaming and his thin mouth twisted with hatred, he attacked. When the Mexicans spied him they often yelled, "Watch out. It's Geronimo!" With this new nickname, Geronimo would become the most feared of all Apache warriors.

Many Mexicans died at Arizpe. "Over the bloody field," exclaimed Geronimo, "covered with the bodies of Mexicans, rang the fierce Apache war-whoop." Still the young warrior desired more revenge. Through the 1850s and 1860s Geronimo led raiding parties into Mexico many times.

In the United States other Apaches, especially the

Mangas Coloradas

Victorio

chiefs, Mangas Coloradas, Cochise, and Victorio, resisted the invasion of their homelands. The discovery of gold brought miners and prospecters streaming into the territories. The U.S. Army built forts to protect them, and soon farmers and ranchers also claimed Indian lands as their own. Lawless pioneers often killed the Apaches, whom they considered savages. Furious Apaches avenged these murders by killing peaceful settlers.

As the two cultures clashed and the Apache raids increased, settlers demanded a solution. Under a flag of truce, soldiers captured and killed Mangas Coloradas. Near Camp Grant, vicious settlers massacred hundreds of friendly Apaches who were camped there under the protection of the U.S. Army. By murder and treachery the homesteaders hoped to wipe out the Apaches.

12

The government's cruel and costly Indian policy deeply disturbed President Ulysses S. Grant. "This policy," an official 1871 report revealed, "has resulted in a war which, in the last ten years, has cost a thousand lives and over forty millions of dollars, and the country is no quieter...." Grant formed a Board of Indian Commissioners to look after Indian affairs. Soon Congress voted money for "collecting the Apaches of Arizona and New Mexico upon reservations." By providing them with food, clothes, and farming tools, the government expected the Apaches to give up raiding and adopt the white man's way of life.

Under the command of General George Crook, the U.S. Army relentlessly battled the warring Apaches until many exhausted bands surrendered. In February 1873 even Cochise agreed to settle on lands in the Dragoon and Chiricahua mountains of southern Arizona. By treaty, the U.S. government promised the Chiricahua Apaches this land for all time. There among its pine forests and gurgling streams, Cochise spent his last days in peace.

After the death of Cochise in 1874, relations between Apaches and whites grew strained again. The government agents running the reservations often cared little about the Indians' welfare. Greedy government contracters provided the Apaches with rotten meat to eat. In the winter these swindlers handed out thin blankets or none at all, and the Indians froze. Cheated again and again, the Apaches silently endured.

The thought of wasting good land on savage Indians angered many heartless white settlers. To meet their demands in 1875, the government broke its treaties. U.S. soldiers marched the Apaches north into central Arizona. With their cool and love-ly mountains stolen from them, the Chiricahua Apaches crowded together with other Apache groups on the dry, treeless plains of the San Carlos Reservation. One sympathetic soldier, Lieutenant Britton Davis, called San Carlos "Hell's Forty

Apache youths playing a ring game at San Carlos Reservation

John Clum with
Apaches of the
San Carlos
Reservation

Acres." Still, reservation agent John Clum tried his best to treat the Indians fairly. He selected leading chiefs to become judges in the reservation court system and enforced reservation laws by training loyal Apaches as police. San Carlos, however, remained a cheerless place where the Apaches felt like prisoners.

Geronimo refused to live at San Carlos. Along

with other warriors he continued his marauding ways, stealing horses and creating an uproar among the settlers. In the spring of 1877 Geronimo's band stopped to rest at the Warm Springs, New Mexico, reservation of the Mescalero Apaches. When John Clum learned this news he rode four hundred miles to capture the Apache band.

On the morning of April 21, 1877, Geronimo and six other fully armed renegades defiantly confronted Clum at the Warm Springs agency. Nervously Clum observed that Geronimo stood "erect as a lodge-pole pine, every outline of his...form indicating strength, endurance, and arrogance." The tough Apache stared at Clum and the twenty-two Apache policemen that stood with him on the agency porch. "We are not going to San Carlos with you," angrily declared Geronimo, "and unless you are very careful, you and your Apache police will not go back to San Carlos either. Your bodies will stay here...to make food for coyotes." As Geronimo's thumb edged toward the hammer of his rifle, Clum touched the brim of his hat. This signal instantly brought eighty additional armed policemen springing from the agency cookhouse. Outwitted and surrounded, Geronimo unhappily surrendered his weapons and became Clum's prisoner.

Geronimo was chained in the San Carlos guardhouse until Clum was removed from duty four months later. More bitter than ever, Geronimo stiffly walked out into the sunshine. It was a time of great hardship for the Apaches. After Clum's departure thieving government agents again ran the San Carlos Reservation. "We were treated very badly by the Agents," Geronimo later claimed. Rather than accept starvation and sickness, he and several hundred other Chiricahua Apaches fled south to the Sierra Madre mountains in 1881.

Frantically the War Department ordered General Crook once more to campaign against these outlaws. To adapt his army to the Arizona countryside,

Apache prisoners in chains

General Crook with Indian scouts

Crook ordered the use of hardy pack-mules instead of great, creaking wagons to carry supplies. While on patrol the mules could climb the steepest mountain trails. To defeat Apache hit-and-run fighting methods, Crook hired trustworthy reservation Apaches as scouts. Only Apaches, he correctly guessed, were skilled enough to catch outlaw Apaches.

Fortunately for Crook, one tired renegade named Tsoe returned to the reservation and surrendered to the soldiers. Tsoe knew where Geronimo was hiding and agreed to lead General Crook there. With a small army of soldiers and scouts, Crook soon crossed into Mexico. As the expedition approached

General Crook's expedition before it left for Mexico

the Sierra Madres, Captain John G. Bourke observed, "On each hand were the ruins of abandoned hamlets, destroyed by the Apaches. . . .The sun glared down pitilessly, wearing out the poor mules. . .slipping over loose stones or climbing rugged hills. . . ." The mountain trails proved so steep and narrow that five mules plunged over cliffs to their deaths. With Tsoe's help, however, Crook at last reached the Apaches' secret camp in May 1883.

Astounded to find their hiding place discovered, the Apache women and children at the camp surrendered. Each following day more renegades stepped from the wilderness and surrendered to Crook. Finally even Geronimo admitted his defeat. Years of fighting Americans and Mexicans had crushed the spirits of most Apaches. Surely life on the reservations, they decided, would be easier than resisting further. By February 1884 most of the Apache outlaws had been captured.

In fact, under General Crook's control, reservation life improved. Allowed to live in a region called Turkey Creek in the White Mountains, the Chiricahua Apaches found clear water, pleasant pine forests, and plenty of deer and other wildlife. Half-heartedly Geronimo tried to become a farmer.

Most Apaches learned to accept the forced changes in their lives. In time, however, Geronimo and others grew restless again. These last stubborn, and proud, Chiracahua Apaches resented the army rules that interfered with Apache customs. In boredom they drank Tizwin, a native alcoholic drink made from corn. The liquor only made the captive Indians more discontented. Threatened with punishment for illegal drinking, Geronimo, Naiche (the son of Cochise), and over one hundred other Chiricahua warriors, women, and children fled Turkey Creek on May 17, 1885.

"The Apaches are out!" raced the news across the telegraph wires. The hostile Indians dashed southward ambushing settlers and stealing horses. As the army chased after distant clouds of dust, soldiers discovered the bodies of seventeen civilians.

Throughout the summer of 1886 the Apaches ranged through the Sierra Madres running, riding, fighting, and hiding. A raid into New Mexico by an outlaw band led by Josannie in November left thirty-eight more ranchers and soldiers dead. To insure the safety of U.S. citizens General Crook again crossed the border.

Not until January 9, 1886, did Crook's Apache scouts find Geronimo's camp. In a surprise attack the army captured all of the renegades' horses and supplies. Immediately Geronimo realized his hopeless situation. On March 25 he met General Crook

Geronimo's camp in Mexico

Geronimo poses with his warriors (top) and with Naiche (bottom).
Both photographs taken after the surrender.

near the U.S. border at the Canyon de los Embudos. Sitting on the ground together beneath cottonwood and sycamore trees, Crook eyed the old warrior. "...why did you kill innocent people," he harshly demanded, "sneaking all over the country to do it?...You promised me in the Sierra Madres that peace should last, but you have lied about it." And, forgetting that the Indians had been lied to countless times by Americans, Crook demanded Geronimo surrender.

Geronimo surrendered to General Crook.

At last Geronimo and the other Apache leaders with him reluctantly agreed. "Once I moved about like the wind," Geronimo solemnly stated. "Now I surrender to you and that is all." The Apache wars appeared to be over. The Apaches slowly followed Crook back toward the United States, escorted by a party of soldiers and scouts. However on the night of March 28, Geronimo changed his mind. Enflamed by liquor provided by a corrupt trader, he slipped away from the escort taking half his band with him.

After a few days of peace, fearful Americans excitedly called again for the immediate capture of Geronimo. At the White House, President Grover Cleveland angrily demanded he be hung. Frustrated and embarrassed, General Crook resigned from his post. General Nelson Miles quickly took command in Arizona and assembled 5,000 troops, a quarter of the entire U.S. Army. With this huge force, Miles started military operations against Geronimo's little band of forty. On mountaintops soldiers constructed a network of heliograph stations whose brightly flashing mirrors allowed fast communication in Morse code. Dust-covered troops of cavalry crisscrossed the Arizona desert. By guarding every known waterhole and mountain pass, they hoped to find and kill Geronimo.

Large army patrols, spurs and sabers jingling,

General Miles constructed heliograph stations for fast communication between the troops.

rarely glimpsed the swift and stealthy Indians. Years later one soldier recalled that chasing after the Chiricahua Apaches was "like chasing deer with a brass band."

However, Geronimo admitted that "contrary to our expectations, the United States soldiers. . .were soon trailing us and skirmishing with us almost every day. Four or five times they surprised our camp." On each occasion the Apaches safely scrambled away, but the constant pressure exhausted them.

On August 23, 1886, Lieutenant Charles B. Gatewood sent two Apache army scouts, Kayihtah and Martine, into Geronimo's mountain camp. "The troops are coming after you from all directions," Kayihtah warned. Their "aim is to kill every one of you if it takes fifty years. . . .everything is against you. . . . If you are awake at night and a rock rolls down the mountain or a stick breaks, you will be running. . . .You even eat your meals running. You have no friends whatever in the world." Gravely Geronimo realized these messengers told the truth. Finally he agreed to meet General Miles.

On September 3, 1886, Miles and his army escort rode through the craggy mountain rises of Skeleton Canyon in southern Arizona. From his nearby

Kayihtah (above left) and Martine (right) led Lieutenant Gatewood to Geronimo's camp. Naiche and Geronimo (right) photographed at Fort Bowie.

mountain camp, Geronimo proudly rode down to meet the old soldier. After the two men shook hands, an interpreter began, "General Miles is your friend."

"I never saw him," Geronimo quietly joked, "but I have need of friends. Why has he not been with me?"

General Miles gazed at Geronimo with the respect of one soldier for another. "He was one of the brightest, most resolute, determined looking men that I have ever encountered," remarked the general. ". . .Every movement indicated power. . .and determination." Miles then stated his surrender terms: "Lay down your arms and come with me to Fort Bowie, and in five days you will see your families. . .and no harm will be done you." He insisted the warriors be sent to Florida for two years' punishment. There, he promised, they would live safely and in comfort. Years of broken promises had taught Geronimo not to trust the white men. Tired and lonely, however, he and his warriors decided to take one more chance.

The next day Geronimo formally surrendered to General Miles. "We placed a large stone on the blanket before us," the Apache leader recalled. "Our treaty was made by this stone, and it was to last till the stone should crumble to dust; so we made the treaty, and bound each other with an oath. . . ."

Guardhouse at Fort Bowie

"I will quit the warpath," promised Geronimo, "and live in peace hereafter."

The last Apache war had ended. Americans sighed with relief as they learned of the capture of the feared and hated Geronimo.

To break the wild spirit of the Chiricahua Apaches forever, Miles unfairly ordered the entire tribe—outlaw raiders, peaceful women and children, and even loyal scouts—into exile. Soon Geronimo traveled eastward by train. For two years he and other leaders remained imprisoned in the stone fortress of Fort Pickens, Florida. Finally in 1887 the government reunited these prisoners with their families at the Mount Vernon Barracks in Alabama. However, it was a sad reunion. "We were not healthy in this place," Geronimo declared, "for the climate disagreed with us." The Apaches suffered dreadfully from heat and disease. In fact, an army report in

Apache prisoners, including Geronimo, in transit to Florida.

1889 revealed that the southern climate and eastern diseases had killed nearly a quarter of the Apaches.

In 1893 the government moved the Chiricahua Apaches again. On the grassy plains near Fort Sill, Oklahoma, the Apache prisoners lived in greater comfort. They plowed the soil and raised melons, cantaloupes, and corn. They herded cattle. Artist E.A. Burbank visited Fort Sill in 1897 to paint a portrait of Geronimo. He described the Apache as "an elderly Indian...short, but well built and muscular. His keen shrewd face was deeply furrowed with strong lines. His small black eyes were watery, but in them there burned a fierce fire."

Geronimo and visitors at St. Louis World's Fair

In his old age, Geronimo accepted invitations to several national expositions. There, in special booths, he sold autographed photographs and handmade bows and arrows to curious visitors. At the St. Louis World's Fair in 1904 the amazed Apache rode on a ferris wheel. The passage of time had thrust Geronimo into America's modern age.

Still Geronimo longed for freedom and the old Apache ways of life. In a meeting with General Miles, Geronimo asked to be allowed to return to Arizona. "The acorns and piñon nuts, the quail and the wild turkey, the giant cactus and the [pines] — they all miss me."

"A beautiful thought, Geronimo," responded Miles. "...But the men and women who live in Arizona, they do not miss you.... Folks in Arizona sleep now at night, [and] have no fear that Geronimo will come and kill them."

In 1905 Geronimo rode in Theodore Roosevelt's inaugural parade. "Hooray for Geronimo!" yelled the crowds as they spotted the stern old warrior. They knew the stories of his ruthless warfare, but they cheered his tough fighting spirit. But not even President Roosevelt would let Geronimo and the Chiricahua Apaches return to Arizona. "We are vanishing from the earth," mourned Geronimo as he watched his people slowly die and his culture disappear.

In February 1909, having lived into his eighties, Geronimo made his final surrender. Falling from his horse after a drinking spree, he lay chilled all night in the frosty grass. On February 17 he died of pneumonia. Soon after, Indians and soldiers silently watched his burial at Fort Sill.

"I want to go back to my old home before I die," Geronimo had said in 1908. "Tired of fight and want to rest. Want to go back to the mountains again." At last in 1913 the U.S. government permitted Fort Sill's surviving Chiricahua Apaches to move to the Mescalero Apache reservation in New Mexico. Taking root again in this familiar countryside, the Apaches, with their proud memories of Geronimo, kept their heritage alive.

Other Americans never forgot him either. During World War II, U.S. paratroopers jumped from planes over enemy territory. To fill their hearts with courage and strike fear into their foes, they fiercely shouted a single word: "Geronimo!"

Geronimo and family in melon patch at Fort Sill

PHOTO CREDITS

Arizona Historical Society—2, 7, 9, 12 (2 photos),
14, 15, 17, 18, 19, 21, 22 (2 photos), 23, 25 (2
photos), 26 (2 photos), 28, 29, 30 (2 photos)

Culver Pictures—1

Fort Sill Army Museum—4, 11, 32

Front cover: *Geronimo* by Henry Farney,
courtesy of Fenn Galleries, Santa Fe, New Mexico

About the Author

Zachary Kent grew up in Little Falls, New Jersey, and received an English degree
from St. Lawrence University. Following college he worked at a New York City liter-
ary agency for two years and then launched his writing career. To support himself
while writing, he has worked as a taxi driver, a shipping clerk, and a house painter.
Mr. Kent has had a lifelong interest in American history. Studying the U.S. presidents
was his childhood hobby. His collection of presidential items includes books, pictures,
and games, as well as several autographed letters.

J B GERONIMO
Kent, Zachary.
The story of Geronimo
$11.95